San Francisco :

EDWARD BOSQUI & CO.,

PRINTERS.

POEMS.

BY

CHARLES WARREN STODDARD.

SAN FRANCISCO:
A. ROMAN AND COMPANY.
1867.

CONTENTS.

IDYLLIC AND LEGENDARY—

OF THE HEART—

OF FANCY AND IMAGINATION—

OF ASPIRATION AND DESIRE—

OF MEDITATION—

INDEX TO ILLUSTRATIONS.

INVOCATION.

OH, Poesy! exquisite gift,
Thou art a magnet that shall lift
My gold from out the drossy rift.

Thou art my soul's refulgent beam
My guiding star to ever gleam
A flaming pillar in my dream.

Thou art my drifting-cloud by day
Whose bright pavilion-courts alway
Allure me with their fair display.

Thou art a Hebe that presents
A chalice to my lips, and thence
I drain the charméd, rich contents.

Delicious, bubbling nectars twine
Their trickling tendrils as a vine
Through all my being; steept in wine

And numb to any thought of earth
I wrestle with my spirit's mirth
In travail with a poem's birth.

When chasing cares are wearying
With all my life to thee I cling—
Believing I was born to sing.

Lo! thou hast taught me where to fly
Escaping every ill; for I,
Transfigured by thy witchery,

As Daphne in the laurel park
Seem wholly shut in leafy ark,
I feel beneath my rugged bark

A nervéd pulse that never cowers;
The turgid stream of sap hath powers
That shall beget a thousand flowers.

I quiver from my very root,
I strive to doff my leafy suit
And load my boughs with perfect fruit—

And lift my gnarled limbs to thee—
I writhe and struggle to be free
Endowed with thy divinity.

Thou art my fast and feast; and true
Thou art my sweetest twilight-dew,
That grants me purer life anew.

And as the flower unto the moon
Returns its hoarded sweets full soon,
I yield thee all, in verse and tune.

Of Nature.

AT POINT LOBOS.

CLEAR noon without obscurity.
No flake of cloud 'twixt heaven and me;
No mist athwart the Golden Gate:
The hearty sun doth wilfully
His profuse beams precipitate.

I cling to humpéd rocks that kneel
On unswept sands, where breakers reel
    In splendid curves, and pile their foam
In spongy hills, that slow congeal,
    And dulce and drift-wood find a home.

We clasp the silver crescent set
Within the hazy parapet
    That belts the horizon: in glee
I count the fitful puffs that fret
    The eternal levels of the sea.

I watch the waves that seem to breathe
And pant unceasingly beneath
    Their silken coverings, that cringe,
As flecked with swirls of froth, they seethe,
    And whip, and flutter to a fringe.

Brown pipers run upon the sand
Like shadows; far out from the land
    Gray gulls slide up against the blue;
One shining spar is sudden manned
    By squadrons of their wrecking crew.

My city is beyond the hill;
I cannot hear its voices shrill:
    I little heed its gains and greeds:
Here is my song, where waters spill
    Their liquid strophes in the reeds.

And to this music I forswear
Whatever soils the world with care:
    I see the listless waters toss—
I track the swift lark through the air—
    I lie with sunlight on the moss.

White caravans of cloud go by
Across the desert of bright sky,
    And burly winds are following
The trailing pilgrims, as they fly
    Over the grassy hills of spring.

What Mecca are they hastening to?
What princess journeying to woo
    In the rich Orient? I am thrilled
With spice and odor they imbue—
    I feed upon their manna spilled!

I strip my breast with eager mind,
To tarry and invite the wind
    To my embrace: by curious spell
It quickens me with praises kind—
    'Tis Ariel that blows his shell!

Invisible, and soft as dews
Descending, he his love renews,
    Delighting daisy colonies
That gloss them with the lustrous ooze
    Of meadows steeped in ecstacies.

Until the homely, sunburnt Heads,
The tumbling hills, in browns and reds,
    And gray sand-hillocks, everywhere
Are buried in the mist that sheds
    Its subtle snow upon the air.

And Prospero, aroused from sleep,
Recalls his spirits from the deep—
    They cross the wave with stealthy tread,
Their shadows down upon me sweep—
    And day is past, and joy is fled.

I hear the dismal bells that shout
Their warning to the ships without:
    The dripping sails are reefed and furled,
The pilots sound and grope about—
    The Gate is barred against the world!

IN CONFERENCE.

IF I could fly the hateful town,
  And flying, suddenly discover
Some velvet valley, softly brown,
  With hills that elbow one another—

Those robust hills: so resolute
  And satisfied, with brawny shoulders
Set close together, in their mute,
  Firm way, that startles us beholders,

And gathered close about my vale,
  To nurse it, sitting still together,
Its body-guard in autumn mail,
  Like Arabs in their cloaks of leather.

I would dispose myself among
  Their surging waves of grain, beseeching
Some brief translation of their tongue,
  Some knowledge of their healthful preaching.

O! pleasure for a spirit vext,
  A listening, after introduction,
To whispered echoes of their text,
  And volumes of their pure instruction;

While ever from the valley's rim
  The wind peeps over as it passes,
And merrily and mild for him,
  Blows silver clouds across the grasses;

Brings down an apple with his hail—
  Plump skin—was ever apple riper?
And frights, in hasty whirr, a quail
  That was my musical chief piper.

Full-bosomed quail in mottled casque
  And plume, and silken bib to cover
Your panting throat, I only ask,
  Return again unto your lover!

Now swoops an inky cloud of birds
  Into the valley's deepest dimple;
They storm me with their teasing words,
  Yet please me with their gambols simple.

I wish those five in epaulets
  Of rose would quell the boisterous greeting;
But I suppose each one forgets
  He interrupts my quiet meeting.

Their little hearts with song-delight
  Are over-full—sufficient reason;
The pretty things are pardoned quite
  For only singing out of season.

Was that a sprinkle on my face,
  Descending from this sky of blueness?
Baptism in this holy place
  Is fitting; for a sense of newness

Pervades these vestibules of earth—
  Sacristies, most securely hidden—
These halls, appropriate to new birth,
  Where all unto the feast are bidden.

How silent has the valley grown—
  The birds have hushed their playful riot;
A mutter, as a bee's dull drone,
  Is all that stirs the perfect quiet.

Transparent curtains of the rain
  Are sweeping down to me, delighting
The dusty trees ; where I have lain
  The broken grasses now are righting.

The swarms of blackbirds lift away ;
  The most demoralized of creatures
Myself will be, if I delay—
  So now, farewell, my wholesome preachers.

With your broad foreheads in the mist,
  You cannot show a sign of sorrow ;
But you are honest, keep the tryst—
  I'll worship with you on to-morrow.

THROUGH THE SHADOWS.

ALL in a dream i' the twilight,
Glimmering stars in their glee,
List to the murmur of far-off
Ripples of tropic sea.

Low in the westward bleeding
The sun slowly sinks in the wave—
Staining and tinting with crimson
The corals that fashion his grave.

Out through the mist and the vapor,
The cloudy wreaths and the rings,
Sunlight has flown like a butterfly
Brushing the gold from its wings.

Quiet is coming and folding
Our troubles away; and our woes
Are hushed in the cool, fragrant shadows,
Like bees in the heart of a rose.

Come on little stars all silver,
  For the terrible sun has gone,
And out of the eastern shadows
  The moon setteth sail for the dawn.

Pale are the stars—for the morning
  Is blooming fresh as the May;
So through the shadows we wander,
  Seeking the perfect day.

THE GUTTER—A CITY IDYL.

YOU are welcome, dusky cloud,
  With your bosom swelling;
And your tears—their patter cheers
  All my dusty dwelling:

And the gutter sudden wakes
  In a thousand voices;
O, the song that rings along
  Where the rill rejoices!

I am happy for the sight,
  Joining your carouses,
Brook and I go laughing by
  All the dripping houses.

You'll excuse us for the noise,
  And our haste and flurry?
We must fly, for soon we die,
  That is why we hurry.

I am here because I like
  Just this sort of weather ;
Brook takes me for company—
  Down we go together.

Ha ! this life's a merry one,
  Though a thoughtless scorner
Cries, "The tomb is full of gloom,
  Down upon the corner."

What if all its life is brief—
  Born of such a shower—
Running through a block or two,
  Dying in an hour ?

There is something still beyond—
  Death is nothing surer—
Brook will flow, and ever grow
  Softer, sweeter, purer,

Till the sun doth draw it hence,
  T'wards its quenchless taper ;
It will rise into the skies
  As a silver vapor.

As it floateth in the air—
  Merciful its slumber—
Then again is born the rain
  Of that cloud of umber.

But the brook is growing still—
  Is the rain abating!
In a breath will sudden death
  Take it at the grating.

You would hardly know it now
  For its faintest mutter—
A shriveled tongue that laps among
  The cobbles in the gutter.

VESPERS.

THE poppies nod their sleepy brows,
And reel adown the opiate air;
The somber lilies slowly rouse,
And fold transparent hands in prayer.

The climbing roses whisper soft
Sweet messages; the four-o'clocks
Are drowsy now—but far aloft
I see the watchmen-hollyhocks.

The Moslem-lilacs seem to call
On "Allah" through the red sunset;
They rise upon the turret-wall
Of every leafy minaret.

The stately tulips at this hour
Forget their pride. With good intent
The haughty dahlias yield their dower—
The dusky peony-queens relent.

A thousand lights are swung in view
  From heaven's dome. I leave the fair
Meek violets kneeling in the dew;
  It is the evening hour of prayer.

BY THE BROOK.

DOWN across the hill's low brow—
A slender, silver fillet—
Nothing is so musical
As my little rillet.
Ah! that laughing song of yours!
Delicately trill it.

Shall I fret you, hasty brook?
Shall I mar your paces—
Weaver, weaving silver threads
Into silver laces,
Round about and in and out
The sunniest of places?

Loose your tresses in the chase,
Slip about the border
Of yon garden wall, and catch
A blossom, gay marauder!
What shall please my love of ease
As your sweet disorder?

While the world goes jogging on,
Presently I miss you;
Life is made of other stuff
Than your limpid tissue.
Turn a mill, you lazy rill,
While I wait the issue.

Let the beetle while away
The Summer with its drumming,
Foam you at the whirling wheel,
And babble to its humming.
Toil away the livelong day—
It is more becoming.

Creep beneath the sweeping bough,
While each ripple twinkles,
Starlike, in a sky of leaves,
And your frothy crinkles
Form a leathern apron there,
Full of creamy wrinkles.

When the bald and brazen day
Hath donned his dusky visor,
Still you flow a-down apace,
While night's myriad eyes are
Watching you; for what they view
No one is the wiser.

YO-SEMITE.

INNUMERABLE lessons to relate
  And myriad voices rushing to baptize
  These chosen lips, which send into the skies
  Their oracles, to awe and elevate.
The world's chief mouth-piece is this marvelous gate,
  That lavish nature wholly sanctifies
  With majesty and beauty. Here my eyes
  Some revelation seem to penetrate;
For God, begetting mysteries from the first,
  All glorified, stood down upon the rock,
  And smiting through, the curious earth was riven—
A thousand silver arteries were burst—
  The mountains staggered from the fearful shock,
  With heart laid bare to the soft eyes of Heaven.

DUSK.

SMOLDERING in heat
  Beyond the blue hill,
His mission complete,
At the Deity's feet,
  When the evening is still,
The Sun, prone and lowly,
  At Angelus kneeling;
  But partly revealing,
Yet not hiding wholly
A shrine and Christ crucified,
  Borne aloft tenderly,
With lovers side by side
  Telling a rosary.

In the violet East,
  All dripping with dew,
Above the long, high,
Purple mountains, that lie

By the vail of the night
And the valley of dreams,
Half dark and half light,
With a flood of bright beams,
The moon steals in view.
The murmur has ceased
In the field and the forest;
The bee and the bird
No longer are heard;
The flocks are not bleating;
My cares that were sorest—
My pains that were fleeting,
Are gone, or at rest;
As blessings entreating,
I linger repeating
My "Ave Maria"—so happy, so blest,
With cross on my forehead and cross on my breast.

THE BUTTERFLY.

THOU little beauty, wafted by
Upon the summer's gentle sigh;
  What art thou? Tell me, pray!
A sunbeam wandering from the sky,
  That earthward found its way?

A gorgeous flower, too rudely blown?
A beautiful bright birdling, flown
  From some enchanted coast—
A winged mosaic, that hath known
  More art than man can boast?

Spring's sudden flying brought to view
Thy form, among the moss that grew
  Along the garden wall;
I saw thee as thou didst renew
  The fleeces of thy pall.

And from the homely commonplace
Of thy crude life I now can trace
  Thy fair and wondrous powers;
I learn the secret of the grace
  That brightens my dull hours.

When folded in the noiseless gloom—
Lo! the shut portals of thy room
  At last were opened wide—
Sunlight had cleft the sealéd tomb
  Where beauty did abide.

May not the homely thought we find
Among the rudest of our kind
  Yet serve an end complete,
If chance it be but choicely lined,
  As was thy winding sheet?

For so a poem will forsake
Its little hiding cell, to wake
  In life's delicious pain,
When sunshine of the heart shall break
  The chrysalis of the brain.

IN THE DESERT.

I.

BEDOUIN IN AMBUSH.

SEVEN hawks, in dismal disarray,
Across a sky of slaty gray,
Now dusking with the dusking day.

The sun low down, and almost hid
Beneath a vapory, dull lid,
Over against a pyramid.

One cluster of incessant green,
Three slender palms that tower and lean—
A crouching sentinel between.

No hissing breath upon the lip—
No stir in poised knee and hip—
No quiver from the finger tip;

But, pointing from the fatal lair,
The lithe wrist glued about the bare,
Dull-gleáming rifle's livid glare.

And slow, with wearisome slow limb,
A caravan approaching him
With fringe of shadows long and slim.

* * * * * *

II.

BEDOUIN ÁBROAD.

A sky of glimmering, cool steel,
But barely serving to reveal
The desert where the camels kneel.

An awkward buzzard on the wing ;
Above one star in filmy ring ;
While lower ranks are hovering

By pots of delicate, spiced flesh ;
Abundant fruits in silken mesh ;
And jars of oil, and olives fresh ;

And costly vestments of the Kahn,
Despoiled with bloody mare and man—
The remnants of a caravan.

Against the sky-rim, silvery,
One motionless, tall cocoa-tree;
The pyramids in angles three.

And yonder, where the morning lowers,
The fleet-winged flying-horseman scours
T'ward Ghizeh and her shining towers.

SUMMER EXODUS.

TURNS Summer hence her queenly feet,
That early spring the daffodils
To kiss, and martial grasses greet,
While every flower a tear distills.

I cross the stubble fields, all sweet
With shining stalks; a longing fills
My heart, to warble and repeat
The robin in his liquid trills.

I am, too, happy when I meet
The meadow, where the mountain spills,
So lithe and musical and fleet,
Its limpid tress of brawling rills;

But stay my solitary beat—
And start, as sudden odor thrills
My brain, of spice and tropic heat—
Lo! Autumn on her brazen hills.

THE FIRST RAIN.

BETWEEN the ranks of thistle, down the road,
The phantom flocks of sunbeams hastily,
With gilded feathers of the butterfly,
Disperse away; anon a weary load
Of grain, wild scented, being freshly mowed,
Comes smoking on; as from the brooding sky
There fall deliberate, still showers of shy,
Big rain-drops all around. The teamsters goad
The swaying oxen, steaming, to a shed
For covering. The brown and dusty trees
Are whispering, as eagerly they spread
Their branches in the rain, and stand at ease,
And listen, yonder in the clover bed
The happy buzzing of ten thousand bees!

TAMALPAIS.

HOW glorious thy dwelling place!
    How manifold thy beauties are!
I do not reckon time or space—
I worship thy exceeding grace,
    And hasten, as a flying star,
    To reach thy splendor from afar.

The first flush of thy morning face
    Is dear to me; thy shadowless,
    Broad noon that doth all sweets confess;

But fairer is thy even fall,
When seem to cry with airy call
  Thy roses in the wilderness.
Thy deserts blithely blossoming,
Decoy me for the love of Spring.
With all thy glare and glitter spent,
Thy quiet dusk so eloquent;
    Thy vail of vapors—the caress
      Of Zephyrus, right cool and sweet—
    I cannot wait to love thee less—
I cling to thee with full content,
      And fall a dreaming at thy feet.

    Anon the sudden evening gun,
    Awakes me to the sinking sun
And golden glories at the Gate.
    The full, strong tides, that slowly run
Their sliding waters modulate
To indolent soft winds that wait
    And lift a long web newly spun.
I see the groves of scented bay,
    And night is in their fragrant mass.

But tassel-shadows swing and sway,
And spangles flash and fade away
    Upon their glimmering leaves of glass—
And there a fence of rail, quite gray,
    With ribs of sunlight in the grass—
And here a branch full well arrayed
With struggling beams a moment stay'd—
Like panting butterflies afraid.

Lo! shadows slipping down the slope
    And filling every narrow vale,
    The shining waters growing pale—
The mellow-burning star of Hope
And in the wave its silver trope.
    A slender shallop, feather-frail,
    A pencil-mast and rocking sail.
The glooms that gather at the Gate;
    The somber lines against the sky,
    While dizzy gnats about me fly,
    And overhead the birds go by,
      Dropping a note so crystal clear,
      The spirit cannot choose but hear.

The hollow moon, and up between
An oak with yard-long mosses, green
In sunlight, now as dull as crape;
The mountain softened in its shape,
Its perfect symmetry attained—
And swathed in velvet folds, and stained
With dusty purple of the grape.

Idyllic and Legendary.

AT ANCHOR.

A SAILOR by the green home shore,
    When seas are ebbing from his view,
    Doth all his early joys renew:
He sings the songs he sang of yore;

He spies his little cot, he smiles
    With a full joy ne'er felt before—
    He holds that one bare prospect more
Than all the summer of the isles.

The quiet home is his; the trees
    Sprang from the seeds his grandsires laid
    Among the mold; within the glade
The myrtles rustle in the breeze.

Above a treasured little grave,
    His early lost, his first deep woe!
    Not any land that he may know
Beyond the purple of the wave

Hath such a jewel in its breast.
He loves each rock and stream and dell;
'Tis only here he cares to dwell,
'Tis ever here he longs to rest.

This is his home of joy and ease:
And better is the myrtle tomb
Than all the heavy dusks that gloom
The groves of spice beyond the seas.

DRIFTING.

A LARK'S song rippled in the air,
With liquid trill that smote the dawn,
He hastened down the dewy lawn
And found the morning breezes fair;

And half the anchor-cable in,
And half the sails were loosed, and full
Of salty winds; with steady pull
He bade the frothing eddies spin

And whirl about his dripping oar,
As on he sped and joined the bark;
Then from the deck he leaned to mark
The wondrous beauty of the shore.

They seemed as falling scales, his tears,
From blinded eyes, that would not see
How comfort in that home could be,
Though comfort kept him all his years.

High on the yard a sailor sang :
"O ! dusky love beyond the sea !
O ! dusky love that longs for me"—
"And thee," the mocking echoes rang.

"There is a glory in the gale—
An idle dream will suit the calm,
And talk of leafy thatch and palm—
Shall fill the watch with song and tale.

"Lo ! yonder is the star that guides
The mariner ; we lift our hands
About the world, in many lands ;
For what are winds, and what are tides,

"But spirits luring us abroad ?
Rise fragrant isles before our eyes—
A pyre for passion's sacrifice,
Where pleasure is our only god !"

* * * * * *

A hundred trilling songs of larks
A hundred blooming dawns may greet,
But who shall stay the wanderer's feet,
And call his spirit from the dark ?

SINGING SHELLS.

LONG ago! long ago!
'Twas Orpheus caught a pale-pink shell,
With deep, dim chambers neatly twined,
And pearly lined, and pearly lined,
And blew the wind
In music through its hollow halls,
Till all the Echoes of the shore
Cried out with joy, and sought a shell,
And caught the faintly lingering tones
Of Orpheus' music—low as moans—
And drew them in each tiny cell,
While rosy walls of all the halls
Grew merry then; and quickly fell
A murmurous song from every shell.

Long ago! long ago!
'Twas Orpheus tuned the shells to voices;
And all along the pebbled shore
Was music, where was none before,

And now each little one rejoices;
  And every shell a tale doth tell
  How music came with them to dwell;
And all along the pearled shore,
  Though winds do rave and toss the wave,
    And bitter spray is on the land,
  He guards them well, each little shell,
    Who holds the waters in His hand.
So, all along the pearled shore,
'Mid sighing waves, or ocean's roar,
They sing, and sing, forevermore.

THE TWO CLEOPATRAS.

NIGHT is the shadow of that Ethiop queen,
With brow as dark as Night, as richly jeweled
In barbarous ravishment of luxury;
The enchantress of the Cydnus, in her toils
Seeking new pleasures, slaying joys with sighs,
And drowning mirth with her full tide of tears.

Night is the shadow of that Ethiop queen,
In rapturous witchery of beatitude;
Who drank a hundred pearls, immaculate
In their white gloom of glory, and of rare
And fabulous richness. Lo! the haughty queen
Heaped the all-immeasurable wealth
Of treasures rare within a vessel, where,
Breathing a mist of filmy radiance—
A seeming vapor woven of gemmy rays,
That lurked in nebulous folds about the latent,
Limpid, and viewless confines of the vessel—
The copious fund, the teeming store of treasure

Was straight dissolved and lost in the crisp bubbling
And all-devouring properties of acids.
  Then, after this accomplished, did she mingle
With added juices, spice, and redolence
Of various tinctures, a most savory draught.
Her folded fingers held the jeweled verge
Of the clear goblet, from pure ether hewn,
Or some most lucent crystal, delicate,
And laid the gleaming halo of the goblet
Against the amorous volume of her lips,
Where broke the violent fever of her love
In turgid crimsoning, deepening the ripe tint
O' the silky curtains hung about the proud,
Voluptuous tower of her enticing feature.
So, staying the hot current of her blood
In the drowsy syrup, clotted here and there,
And crusted in pearl-ices, glittering pastes,
And frosty miracles of rich congealment
About the invisible limits of the vessel;
Drank she the all incalculable value
Of crystalizing dregs, and hurled the cup
At a dumb serving slave, a fawning eunuch,
Black as hell's border, crouching close along,
The swelling curvature of her fair barge

Heading the vast armada, as it lay
Becalmed among the silver of the Cyndus.
The dense aroma of their several freights
Had quite embalmed the zephyr, and they lay
Beating the silver bosom of the Cyndus,—
Like prisoned birds, with fretful throb of wings,
Beating the bosom of the silver Cyndus,
Close upon Tarsus, where reveled Anthony.

Night is the shadow of that Ethiop queen :
She strews the seas with stars innumerable—
The bubbly sea with stars which are as pearls;
And when the wave is like to stiffen, or burst
Its dusky rind for too great store of rare
And gleaming treasure, Night! lo, haughty Night,
The very shadow of that Ethiop queen
Dips at the borders of the teeming sea
And drinks the richness of the winy flood,
Leaving the world as empty of the dark
And cloudy turbulence of Muscadine
As was the crystal chalice that was drained
By the proud daring of old Egypt's queen.

AT THE SPRING.

I KNEW a cumbrous hill,
From whose green breast did daintily distill
A throbbing rill.

This is the artery,
And further on the crystal heart must be,
Thought said to me.

All other I forsook,
To follow every twist and curious nook
Of this wild brook.

Among deep mosses set,
I found the glimmering fount that did beget
The rivulet.

No other eye had known
Its secret, nor ear heard, for it made moan
Always alone.

I quaffed its waters clear:
Its limpid music babbled to mine ear
With voice sincere.

Then such a silence fell
Upon me, mantling me, as where a spell
Is wont to dwell.

Yet fled I from the place
At a rude rustling: and fear gave me chase
In my disgrace.

'T was a slim water-snake
Slipt like an arrow through the shivering brake,
And left no wake.

But cleft the placid spring
And waved its flaming sword, its forked sting,
In a charmed ring.

* * * * * *

So was the fountain spoiled,
Within its lucid walls a devil coiled—
My trust was foiled.

Of the Heart.

MADRIGAL.

A MAID is sitting by a brook,
The sweetest of sweet creatures :
I pass that way with my good book
Yet cannot read, nor cease to look
Upon her winsome features.

Amid the blushes on her cheek
Her small, white hand reposes :
I am a shepherd, for I seek
That wilful lamb, with fleece so sleek,
Feeding among the roses !

MY LITTLE LOVE.

WHEN my little love at purple dusk,
  Trips out upon the lawn among the flowers,
The blushing roses quiver in their musk,
  Love-smitten through: the feathery, fragrant showers
Of snow-white blossoms drift upon the grass,
Kissing her whispering footsteps as they pass.

When my little love at evening's hush,
  Goes dancing down the dell with laugh and song,
The slumbering echoes waken, and a gush
  Of silvery voices greet her, and along
The dewy clusters of the trailing vines
In music mingles, murmurs, and repines.

When my little love hath sought her cot
  To dream of angels, as the stars grow clear
I homeward plod—alas! unhappy lot—
  Yet turn again—I'd long to tarry near—
Till slowly wandering, thinking of her still,
I meet the blue night coming o'er the hill.

SWEETHEART.

O! THIS love of mine!
Never artist's dream
Was as fair as she:
Jetty locks, that seem
Glossy as can be—
Night before the day
Hath streaked it through with gray.

O! this love of mine!
Brow as white as sands
On a tropic shore;
Eyes as deep as seas
And darker than before
Dawn hath turned them blue;
Cheeks of richest hue,
Pink as pinkest shell
That ever mermaid bore
From enchanted lands

Home where she did dwell.
Sometimes, if I please
That she blossom more,
Her beauty is so fine—
Rosy as red wine.

O! this love of mine!
Mouth a ripened fruit,
If the maid is mute,
Tempting me to sin
In delicious greed;
If a smile I win,
Then with charming speed
It is cleft indeed,
Showing pearly seed.

O! this love of mine!
Such a witching curl,
Such a cunning chin,
Like a single pearl
With a dimple in;
Parian carvéd throat
All of curvéd lines

Such as Psyche shows,
When she sad reclines
In some isle remote
Mourning Cupid's boat
Fading out of view ;
Is the picture true?
Then her bosom's snow
In twin drifts, but hush!—
All that I have shown
Could not bid her blush :
If you are a maid,
Since never was a pair,
Quite too much is said
Unless you are as fair;
If you are a man,
Mate her if you can !

A PROVERB PROVED.

WILL my love's so truthful eyes
  Ever fail me, though I please
From their depths to draw supplies
  That could waste the seas?

Will those pure, delicious springs
  Ever fail me? Wretched day
When my heart no longer brings
  Its life-draught away!

Do they nourish my desire
  But to break the golden bowl:—
At their margin bid expire
  My all-thirsting soul?

No! a voice forever tells
  That my love's so truthful eyes
Are th' unfathomed crystal wells
  Where within truth lies.

Of Fancy and Imagination.

THE SECRET WELL.

I KNOW a well so deep and cool
And hid, the crystal-hearted pool
Hath never thrilled a swallow's throat
    Or sweetened one lark's note.

No fainting stag, though perishing,
Hath ventured to disturb this spring :
No leopard with its fiery breast
    This fountain dares molest.

No cunning, silver-casèd trout
The sheltered source can e'er find out—
No tongue but mine may ever tell
    The secret of this well.

I build about its guarded rim
With added stones ; I know the dim,
Still twilight of its mossy cell
    Where the sweet waters dwell.

For spirits go between us two
With flasks; they brim with softest dew.
I drink and am refreshed, and seem
As living in a dream.

This well, that is alone for me,
Is but a fount of memory:
And every year that I have known
Is but an added stone.

My willing thoughts, as spirits, haste
To draw the draught I love to taste.
There is an ever full supply
Yet who may drink but I?

CHERRIES AND GRAPES.

NOT the cherries' nerveless flesh,
However fair, however fresh,
May ever hope my love to win
For Ethiop blood and satin skin.

Their luster rich and deep their dye;
Yet under all their splendors lie—
That which I cannot tribute grant—
Their hateful hearts of adamant.

I love the amber globes that hold
That dead-delicious wine of gold;
A thousand torrid suns distill
Such liquors as these flagons fill.

Yet tropic gales with souls of musk
Should steep my grapes in steams of dusk:
And orient Eden nothing lacks
To spice their purple silken sacks.

THE WOODPECKER.

A BUSY woodpecker! What would you call
This monk of a fellow, tapping a tree
With little cells like a catacombed hall,
To bury his acorns in—what would you call
Such a curious monk as he?

Tucking his acorns away in their tomb
To feed upon, by and by, at his will—
Does he ever think of the hidden bloom
In the acorn's heart? Though shut in a tomb
There is life cherished there still.

Time is a woodpecker, crowding the cells
Of the catacombed earth with holy dead;
But there's a bud of life that swells
In the oak tree's might and it shatters the cells
As the soul when the life has fled.

NIGHT SONG.

WAS it a corse embalmed in state?
  Was it a princess pale in death,
    White in her bridal vail?
  All of the roses held their breath
And the dews fell very early and late,
    I thought that they never would fail—
While the night went out and the morn came in,
And the drowsy world awoke with a din,
    And the fading stars fled with a wail.

Never a corse in its bleachen shroud,
  Never the daughter of a queen
    Under sarcophagus bars;
  But the fairest face that ever was seen,
Hid i' the misty hem of a cloud—
    Softly the night wind jars
The nebulous texture asunder, and soon
The angel of midnight bore the moon
    Over a flood of stars.

MARS.

NOW Mars steals over the water;
  He is marching down from the sky—
Great Mars with his golden helmet
  And the golden flame in his eye.

The sea is still, for the ripples
  Are hushed at the god's slow tread;
And a line of light is trailing
  The wave like a burning thread.

Sad Mars! he is wearied with marching,
  And wandering off is he,
While he nods his yellow helmet
  And thrusts his lance in the sea.

Faltering Mars! with his marching
  Wearied he seems to be;
While he tips his helmet and merges
  His golden lance in the sea.

THE COMET.

WAS it a star,
Or was it a pearl,
Loosed with a jar
From its setting
I' the coronet moon,
And begetting,
As it fell with a whirl—
Whirling far—
A splendor that faded too soon?

Was it a dream
Of some splendid star born,
That glowed with a gleam
And a quiver
That startled the night?
Like a river
That flowed to the morn
It did seem,
In its luminous, lustrous light.

Was it a gem
Transfixed with a ray
From the burning, bright hem
Of the wondrous,
Terrible sun, or the moon?
Over us, under us,
Nor night, no, nor day
Hath its equal, bright gem
Fair feather of light, flown too soon.

THE ANGEL, THE WINE, AND PEARLS.

AN ALLEGORY OF THE YEAR.

I.

I SAW a tiny flask of wine
An Angel held, 'twas rare and fine.

A little golden round of light,
With every dainty picture dight.

Upon its sculptured sides I found
Both joy and woe, close linked around.

I wondered at the goblet fine,
The gleaming gold, the little wine.

The Angel said; "This flask I hold
Is more to man than simple gold,

"Or rosy nectar; here are found—
Within its fair and golden round—

"Great drops of blood that yield a life
With every dainty pleasure rife;

"Nor lacks it woe at times; and here
Are stored the secrets of a year.

II.

"These pearls"—the Angel's delicate hand
A dozen radiant pearls it spanned—

"Are months, that will the goblet load
Until the rim is overflowed:

"The crimson flood is crowded up
Until the year's end fills the cup."

And having said, the Angel spilled
A single pearl, the inner gild

Was deeper buried in the hue
Of crimson. Said the Angel: "View!

"A pearl is dropped, a time has flown,
The secret of a month is known."

Then fell another; others still
Close followed this, and this, until

The crimson flood rose bubbling up—
Each pearl-drop deeper filled the cup—

And rosily just brimmed the top.
But one more pearl was left to drop.

III.

I looked. Her fingers loosed, it falls—
The round of golden-gleaming walls

Are sunk below the crimson line—
The buried pearl has spilled the wine.

The Angel set the cup aside;
I asked: "Why this?" and quick replied

The radiant spirit, reaching up
To clasp another ready cup:

"Each pearl-month i' the goblet falls,
The life-blood climbs the golden walls

"Until the rim is reached, and here
Is broke the bubble of the year.

"The gems have run the goblet o'er,
The wine is richer for the store:

"The pearls are spilled, the months have flown,
The secrets of a year are known."

SANCTUARY.

SURELY some sacrilegious hand
  Hath robbed the temples of their store
Of relics, up and down the land
  And hurled the altars o'er,

And strewn the treasures all among
  These quiet valleys. As I walk
I find a pearly rosary hung
  Upon this lily stalk.

Hath timid maid, or tearful nun
  Bethought her of this lone retreat
Yet, with her "*Ave*" scarce begun,
  Her prayer-beads at her feet,

Intruders bid her quickly fly,
  And flying, frighted, she forgets
That where she knelt in secret lie
  Her glittering amulets.

Alas ! how poor, how desolate
  The place where man strode rudely by,
The pink no more shall elevate
  Its chalice to the sky.

And here are bleeding roses shorn
  Along the hedge—by shearer vext,
Rare antique rubrics—roughly torn
  From that quaint leafy text.

And thistle-aspergills bestrew
  Meek buds that nestle at their side
With holy drops of luscious dew
  That night hath sanctified.

The morning-glory's fragile cup
  A lucent honey-drop could boast ;
Fair monstrance—it is broken up,
  And vailed is the Host.

And what is this that greeteth me,
  The *Calla*, that I prize above
All lilies? so I mention thee,
  O ! lily of my love—

A perfumed satin altar cloth
  With one tall, golden candlestick;
A velvet butterfly's the moth
  That frets thy rosy wick.

Thy spotless napkin doth enfold
  Such balm and costly frankincense,
As shrouds the swinging censer's gold
  In clouds that struggle thence.

But now I hear the vesper call
  Of floating air-bells, deftly tipt;
The dove's at her confessional—
  The monk-mole in his crypt.

And flowery fields my eyes engage;
  The rivulets, the winding ways—
A missal, whose illumined page
  Is given up to praise.

So if none false hath donned the gown
  And sought the votive priest to play,
Then thrown the sacred altars down
  And hid the charms away—

Dear Nature is the saint that rears
  This sanctuary to our God—
And still renews through all the years
  Where hateful feet have trod.

Of Aspiration and Desire.

DECREES.

I SIT in sorrow by the watery gates,
A questioning the Fates.

I ask: "What manner of strange ships are these
Slipping adown the seas?

"Slipping adown the slanting seas—what sail
Is yonder—calm and pale?"

Then the Fates answer me: "That goodly bark
Braving the waters dark

"So fearlessly—the cross upon her mast—
Is *Trust*, come home at last.

"Yon quivering craft that veers and puts about,
Is the long-cruising *Doubt*.

"This dancing galley that the waters mock,
Shall strike upon the rock;

"'T is *Chance*, a pleasure yacht; her ribs shall bleach
Upon the blistering beach."

Yet still I see a flamelike, shining cloud,
And eager cry aloud:

"That other sail that waits upon the wind—
What is her name and kind?"

To me the Fates: "Though lying still and wan
She shall approach anon;

"So nobly manned—with any gale to cope—
Behold the trusty *Hope*."

"Quicken the winds, I pray you, worthy Fates,
In her are stored my freights!

"Nor am I fit for life of any sort,
Till she shall reach the port."

FAME.

SHE charmed him with her charming eye;
To know its luster was to die,
Or feed forever on its light.
She bore him to her mountain height;
With wine-sweet lips she kissed to rest
The thousand longings in his breast.

She ringed him with her glittering coils;
Her flattering words were soft as oils,
All swam before his drunken sight;
He felt his beauty and his might,
And cursed the darkness as he hurled
Defiance at the crouching world.

He did not know her treachery;
But thought her tightened grasp to be
The clasp of love—O! heavy fate!
She thrust him in the face of hate
With all the venom in her born,
And slew him with her tongue of scorn.

DESIRE.

I WOULD the Fates were busier
  A shaping out my name and story.
    It seems not like a haggard Fate
    To hesitate, and hesitate;
But they'll demur if they prefer,
  And far away is fame and glory.

Perhaps delay is profiting,
  And disappointments shape a moral;
    But age cares not for sweet applause,
    For age is wise with "says and saws."
With merry spring I love to sing
  And with my youth I seek my laurel.

I cannot choose experience
  To lead me faltering and jaded,
    While all the blossom of my life
    Is wasting in the fretful strife,
Till reaching hence that height intense
  I find the myrtle plucked or faded.

No wreath of honor dignifies
  The silver hairs, nor all endeavor
    Finds any mark of royalty
    However rich the trophy be.
Now I would rise and seize the prize,
  Then rest forever and forever.

COMPENSATION.

WHAT if my tender roots may haply coil
    In a deep mellow soil,
    Wherein is found no weed
That killeth all things with its harmful greed,
But only there is nourished mine own reed—
    To rear its slender crest
In every hue of richest blossom dressed?

If in the sunny mazes of my leaves
    The crafty spider weaves—
    Or in my fairest bloom
Some worm hath stole, where in delicious gloom
It lies and fattens in its honeyed tomb—
    What shall it profit me,
The outward show so fair, the prize I seem to be?

Still, I may 'scape the worm, the spider's net;
    No cursed blight may set
    Its dangerous touch anew

Upon my frailest buds, in vile mildew;
My faded flowers the Autumn winds may strew;
        But, after all the strife,
If I have borne no fruit, or seed, what use was life?

UNREST.

O! VESTAL lilies, white and still,
Thy golden cressets newly trim;
O! wine-tipt tulip globes now spill
Thy orient oils upon the flame;
My heavy woe I may not name,
But woe were less if thou wouldst fill
Each golden cresset's rim—
For I may burn within the fire
All bitterness, but what is true
Endures the ordeal of the pyre,
And swathes itself in gossamer dew.

O! summer wind return again
And sing my little ills to rest;
Distill thy balm, delightful rain,
Through various currents of the air;
The cross is heavy that I bear;
But thou mayest lull the vexing pain
And breathe a quiet in my breast.

Peace, weary heart! O! tongue be mute!
  Voluptuous goddess, prithee, weep
Thy golden tears, and soft salute
  Yon star, my soul desireth sleep.

A RHYME OF LIFE.

IF life be as a flame that death doth kill;
  Burn little candle lit for me,
With a pure spark, that I may rightly see
  To word my song and utterly
      God's plan fulfill.

If life be as a flower that blooms and dies;
  Forbid the cunning frost that slays
With Judas-kiss, and trusting love betrays:
  Forever may my song of praise
      Untainted rise.

If life be as a voyage, or foul, or fair:
  O! bid me not my banners furl
For adverse gale, or wave in angry whirl,
  Till I have found the gates of pearl
      And anchored there.

THE AWAKENING.

I TOUCHED the shore in other climes
Encompassed by warm leagues of sea;
I breathed the spicy breath of limes
The sauntering gales bore down to me.

A hundred palms with feathered tips
Displayed their fair pavilion screens
Upon the yellow sandy slips;
Beyond the beating barks were seen.

And as the barks were blown across
The summer-blue of ocean's breast,
My thoughts were borne about to toss
Among the currents of unrest.

My hammock swung within a shade,
I loosed my thoughts where they would rove,
Then sounds were hushed, the ships did fade,
I slumbered in the musky grove.

I dreamed, and all my thoughts returned
  Across the far-dividing deep,
And that dear land for which I yearned
  I seemed to find in fevered sleep.

In dreams I reached my native shore,
  I found the year in deep decline,
The desolate, dull landscape bore
  No hopeful look to answer mine.

I faltered then and prayed for hope—
  And hope is his whoever wills;
With half a hundred doubts to cope
  I strode across the bronze-brown hills.

Then seeking with impulsive haste
  Some phantom that my brain had wrought,
Old, dear familiar streets I paced,
  But missed forever what I sought.

Where were the faces that I knew?
  Where were the hearts that I could trust?
Below the dark and lonely yew
  Was heaped away their hallowed dust.

"O Christ!" I cried, "who died for us
That we might live; one only kiss
From those mute lips!" "Why sorrow thus?
There is another life than this—"

A mellow voice of heavenly calm
With its annunciation spilled
Soft chrism oils, and straight a balm
Fell on me, and my pain was stilled.

But then I pleaded: "Take me hence
To glorify thee and adore,
For what are actions or events
With kindred gone forevermore?"

The voice replied: "No action dies
Although forgotten long, it still
A sure conviction shall arise—
A spirit working good or ill."

Then shame smote crimson down my face,
I hastened from the place of tombs,
A lighter heart bespoke me grace,
I doffed my dismal cloak of glooms.

I cried: "I will rejoice to do
  Such deeds that nothing ill shall dare
To stand erected in the view
  Of the new legend, fresh and fair."

Then swinging in my hammock, hung
  In arbors filled with fine perfume,
My pulses quickened as they sung:
  "We shall anon this task assume."

And swaying with the swaying boughs,
  With odors of the fruit and flowers
About me, tempting me to drowse
  Forever in the scented bower,

There came a voice from out the waves,
  It was not as the voice of men:
"All they that lie in loathed graves,
  They shall arise and live again;

"And whether urns with precious mold,
  Or whether acts long since forgot,
A new shall come of every old,
  There is no death in any lot."

I could have turned as adders turn
  To slay themselves in misery,
That I had lived my life to learn
  So late the worth of life to me.

O! foolish lips that were content
  To sup the honey of soft song!
O! silly heart so sweetly blent
  With harp-like music trilled too long!

O! heavenly oracle divine
  That filled my heart with holy flame,
What new delight of life is mine?
  What miracle of hope and aim?

Of Meditation.

MY FRIEND.

I HAVE a friend who is so true to me,
We may not parted be.

Though I have strayed, on to the uttermost,
Yet is his voice not lost.

If I am madly-deaf for having erred,
Still may I hear his word.

If sin hath slain mine honor, straight appears,
The river of his tears,

Wherein I find redemption ; tenderly
He woos my fear away

And searches out some star of hope, above,
So boundless is his love.

When from the loathéd grave I shall arise,
He 'll hail me from the skies.

Who else would seek me in corruption's dress
With a so kind caress?

Though I am weak, there is a hope of power;
He is my mighty tower;

Like as a flame to fright the gloom away;
He is my perfect day.

I am the homely bulb that tops the reed—
He is the precious seed.

I am the rudest shell the vext-waves whirl—
He is the priceless pearl.

Thou art indeed my friend while ages roll,
O, thou, my deathless soul!

SEED-TIME.

GRIEF is a rain, to fall
Upon us, one and all,
Like needful showers that make the dry earth mellow;
For autumn days will come—
The root of love is numb,
Its sweetest blossoms all are sear and yellow.

And then a quick regret
Will harshly seem to whet
The ploughshare of misfortune, while it burrows
Along its cruel way;
And glossy locks grow gray
And lusterless beside the new-turned furrows.

Old Time comes on amain—
A farmer with his grain,
Experience he sifts between his fingers,
As up and down he goes.
Search, Time, along the rows;
Lest in thy path a weed of evil lingers!

His cunning skill is such
He seeks with careful touch
The seeded groves with softest soil to cover;
Yet, Time, thou hast not art,
But in some bruiséd heart
Long traces of thy husbandry will hover!

O, busy husbandman,
How perfect is thy plan!
Behold the harvest! for thy careful flinging
Of little curious seed
Shall come a crop indeed;
Lo! peace, and trust, and every virtue springing!

PENSEROSA.

IS it sin to deal with sorrow?
  Looking upward through our tears,
    All the breadth of sky is clearer,
    And twice beautiful; and dearer
Seems the coming of the morrow
  As we wrestle with our fears;
Wherefore should we comfort borrow,

While the woe may come again?
  For our little life is brief;
    And though never joy shall light it,
    Truly not our tears shall blight it;
For the Christ once suffered pain,
  And *He* was acquaint with grief—
He, the blessed Christ, did deign

Himself to weep. What matter whether
  Smile or sigh? The fairest bow,

Where the sun the spray hath kissed,
There it blossoms in the mist
Till it withers in fair weather.
Beautiful is grief! I know
Peace and tears may dwell together.

AT POLLOCK'S GRAVE.

ONE seared leaf quivering down
From the green choir that wails thy brief renown :
This is the poet's crown !

Where is thy skillful lute,
That could provoke the birds to sweet dispute ?
Alas ! forever mute !

The hand that drew the balm
Of ravishing music from tuned strings is calm ;
The worm feeds on thy palm.

Not the majestic sweep
Of subtle melodies thy nerve could keep
From out the dusty heap.

The eager sun-rays dart
Through silken grasses, searching for thy heart,
Of perfect gold a part.

The frail vine mantling
Thy undeserved nakedness doth cling
About thee, perishing.

Though no cut altar-stone
Is set to tell these ashes are thine own,
Thou art not all unknown.

Nor dost thou, voiceless, wait;
A thousand whispering tongues shall penetrate
The Heaven's pearly gate:

Singing thine unsung songs,
Chanting thy praises out of tuneful throngs,
And righting all thy wrongs.

* * * *

I would some song dispense,
But falter in my homely utterance,
For music is flown hence.

"DROWNED! DROWNED!"

'TIS said when drowning, snatched from life
and light—
When drowning in sad waters deep and wide—
When drowning, that the waters and the wave
Do moan most musically, and singing, sigh
In tenderest tones, and witching wild refrains,
That enter at the ear and fill the brain
With music, quieting; and that the soul
Is fraught with harmony, and urged to leave
Its transient habitation i' the clay,
And seek that far-beyond, we know not of.

The body's tenantless sleep is all a-cold;
And coming tides slow bear it to the strand,
Among the rushes; and the fingers close
In icy clasp among the rushes, while
The ripples, each in turn, slip up the shore,
And kiss the feet, and close about the hands,
And twine the hair among the roots, and trail

The long sea-grasses over all the form
In slimy ribbons.

Then the tides recede
And leave the body, pale, and lank, and cold,
All in the silence of night, upon the strand—
Sad waters moaning for the still, dead form,
The soulless body sleeping on the strand.
And after
A bleachen skull, outstaring the bold sun—
The mystery of birth, and age, and name—
The secret of the soul's flight, and the blank
And wordless story of a shattered life!

* * * * *

The rattling reeds, and the salt-odored sea
In tireless waves—the hollow autumn wind
Tossing among the rushes—and one star
Dropping pearl shadows in the empty bowls
That held the eyes once in this withered skull!

THE SOUTHERN CROSS.

WHENE'ER those southern seas I sail,
  I find my eyes instinctive turning
Where, pure and marvelously pale,
  Four sacred stars are brightly burning.

A star is set above the thorns;
  Two mark the bleeding palms extended;
And one the wounded feet adorns—
  In four the potent cross is blended.

One only hand had power to place
  The symbol there, and that immortal;
Those fair, celestial fires may grace
  And beautify the heavenly portal.

Whatever danger I may meet
  Upon the wild, disastrous ocean,
Still turn my trusting eyes to greet
  That flaming cross with true devotion.

Nor cease, my willing heart, to give
  Thy prayers, and every just endeavor;
For only by the cross I live,
  And by the cross I live forever.

"*DION.*"

(LYMAN R. GOODMAN.)

YOU sang too early in the spring
Of our uncheerful year of song;
You felt the bitter chill of wrong,
And on a sudden ceased to sing.

And on a sudden sang no more
In skillful measure to our needs;
But there is One who ever heeds
Your numbers on the farther shore.

I picture you as one who lies
  Among the palms, with harp and crown.
  A silver, quivering thread, let down
From crystal walls of Paradise,

Is the sweet echo of your voice
  That thrills me. In your vineyard's throng
  I taste your purple grapes of song,
And in their honey-blood rejoice.

IN MEMORIAM.

L. C. B.

OB. MDCCCLXIV.

ÆT. XXVI.

ONLY now the chrysalis ;
  Only now the mortal clay,
  Cold and breathless, utterly.
What may wake him ? Not a kiss
  On the purest brow I know,
O ! so pallid ; not a kiss
    On the listless, closed eyes ;
    They can look beyond the skies
At the white throne. Not a kiss
  On the hollow cheek of snow.
What shall wake him ? Not a kiss
  On the bloodless, sealed lips,
  For an angel's finger-tips
Ever-silence there have prest ;
And the quiet of his breast
  Is a holy sepulcher ;

And the sleeping Christ within,
Is his heart immaculate,
Purged of every blight and sin.
Death the ashes did inter
With the odor and the balm,
Nourished in the long increase
Of the Christ-man's perfect calm,
And his soul's eternal peace.
Faith and Hope sit at the gate
Of the sepulcher, and wait
For the dawning judgment day;
At the portal while I weep,
At the portal while I pray,
Kneeling at the silent tomb—
Who will break the awful gloom?
Who shall wake him from his sleep?
Who can roll the stone away?

Slumber on and take thy rest;
Peace forever will abide
With thy memory at my side,
Dove-like; and upon my breast
Falls thy spirit sanctified!

Only here the chrysalis,
  Only here the mortal clay,
  Cold and breathless utterly.
Naught may wake him ; not a kiss ;
  Not a kiss or prayer for aye
Shall recall him out of bliss !
Only here the chrysalis,
  With the spirit flown away !

www.ingramcontent.com/pod-product-compliance
Lightning Source LLC
LaVergne TN
LVHW021422110826
845150LV00007B/2034

* 9 7 8 1 4 2 5 5 0 8 7 8 4 *